THE MISSED MEETING

What One Conversation Can Reveal
About Everything Else

PETE KETCHUM

For the leaders who suspect there's a better way.
And for my wife, who believed I could find it.

CONTENTS

ACKNOWLEDGMENTS

This book stands on the shoulders of Edward Deci and Richard Ryan, whose four decades of research on Self-Determination Theory provided the scientific foundation for everything in these pages. Their work proved what good leaders have always sensed: people don't need to be motivated. They need to stop being demotivated.

To the leaders who let me learn these lessons alongside them, sometimes by getting it right, more often by getting it wrong first: the stories in this book are yours, even when the names aren't.

THE ARC MODEL

Three Psychological Needs for Human Motivation

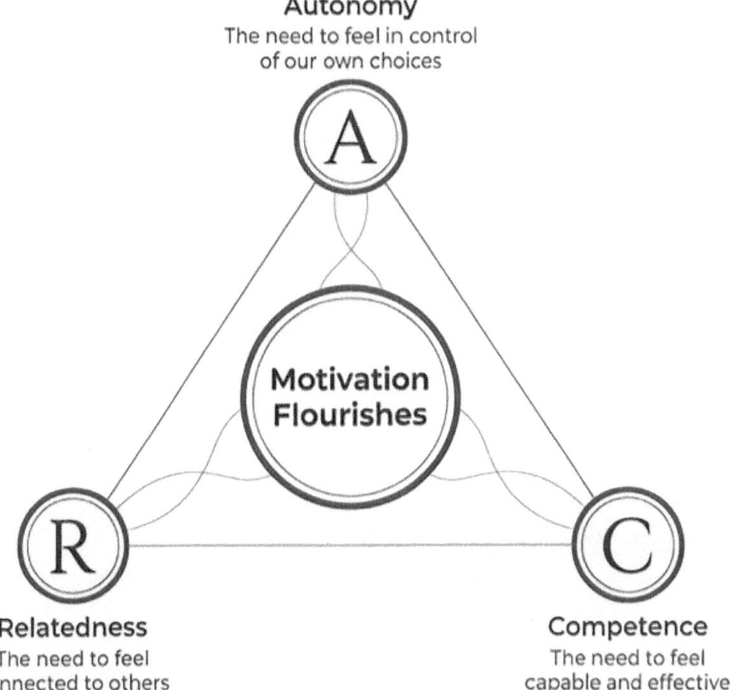

"When these three needs are met, motivation flourishes naturally. When they are blocked, people shut down. It's not a choice they make. It's how humans work."

THE MISSED MEETING

Why the Most Important Meeting in Your Organization Reveals Everything That's Wrong With It

The one-on-one meeting is the most misunderstood thirty minutes in business. Leaders treat it as a status update. Employees treat it as a performance to survive. Both parties leave wondering why they bothered.

But here's what nobody tells you: that awkward silence, that reluctant participation, that sense that you're both going through the motions? That's not a meeting problem. That's your organization's immune system trying to tell you something.

Here's the thing that should trouble every executive: humans come pre-installed with motivation. Most people don't need to be incentivized to do good work. Give them meaningful tasks and reasonable autonomy, and they'll outperform any bonus structure you could design. This isn't wishful thinking. It's psychology.

So why does your workforce feel disengaged? Why did your most enthusiastic hires become your most checked-out employees? Something happened between their first week and now.

The answer isn't bad hires or generational laziness. The answer is that your organization has become exceptionally good at destroying the motivation that was already there. And the one-on-one is where that destruction becomes visible, if you know what to look for.

I call it "the missed meeting" not because it doesn't happen, but because even when it does, it rarely accomplishes what it should.

The meeting becomes a ritual everyone endures rather than a resource anyone values. But here's what most leadership books won't tell you: that friction isn't a meeting problem. It's a signal, a window into everything working against your culture. Before I explain what this signal means and how to read it, I need to tell you about my first spectacular failure. If anyone should have gotten this right from day one, it was me.

THE WRONG OPERATING SYSTEM

I came to leadership through an unusual path. In the military, I trained in interrogation. Not the Hollywood version with bright lights and psychological warfare, but the methodical work of building rapport under pressure, reading resistance, and structuring conversations to get to the truth. From there, I became a de-escalation specialist at a state prison, then a state trooper handling volatile roadside interviews. Every role required the same core skills: establishing trust quickly, maintaining structure under pressure, and following through on commitments.

I later earned a master's in industrial-organizational psychology, adding academic rigor to field experience. I studied what makes people tick in organizational settings. I learned the research on motivation, feedback, and team dynamics. By the time I transitioned to civilian leadership (first in finance, then construction, then tech), I believed I was uniquely prepared to lead teams and would have no problem conducting one-on-one meetings.

I had spent years having difficult conversations with people who didn't want to talk to me. How hard could a thirty-minute check-in with a willing employee be?

It was a Tuesday in late March, my third week as a manager at a mid-sized tech company. I'd scheduled my first round of one-on-ones with my six direct reports, blocking thirty minutes each with the confidence of someone who had no idea what was coming.

The first meeting was in a small glass-walled conference room off the main floor. The kind where everyone walking by can see you but not hear you. I'd printed a one-page agenda: three questions about current projects, two about blockers, and one about career development. I'd even brought a legal pad to take notes, the way I'd been trained to document interviews.

My first report (I'll call her Sarah) arrived two minutes early. She was a well-regarded senior customer service representative with about 3 years at the company. She sat down across from me, laptop closed, hands folded on the table.

"Thanks for making time," I said. "I wanted to use these sessions to understand what's working, what's not, and how I can help remove obstacles."

She nodded.

"So," I continued, glancing at my agenda, "let's start with your current projects. What's taking up most of your bandwidth right now?"

"New customer onboarding," she said.

I waited for more. In an interrogation, silence is a tool. You let it expand until the other person fills it. But Sarah didn't fill it. She just looked at me with an expression I couldn't read.

"How's that going?" I tried.

"Fine."

I wrote "customer onboarding - fine" on my legal pad, then immediately felt ridiculous for writing it.

The next twenty-three minutes were the longest of my professional life. I asked about blockers; she said there weren't any. I asked about collaboration with other teams; she said it was good. I asked about her career goals; she said she was happy where she was. Every question I'd prepared, the same methodical approach that had worked in environments where people actively wanted to deceive me, was producing nothing.

When the timer on my phone buzzed at the twenty-eight-minute mark, I felt relief.

"Okay," I said, already mentally moving on. "Same time next week?"

Sarah paused. Then she said something I still think about years later.

"Do we have to?"

She wasn't rude about it. If anything, she seemed genuinely puzzled, like I'd suggested we meet weekly to watch the paint dry.

I don't remember what I said next. Something about "touching base" and "alignment." She nodded politely and left. Through the glass wall, I watched her walk back to her desk, put on her headphones, and get back to work as if the past half-hour hadn't happened.

The remaining five one-on-ones that week produced variations on the same theme. Polite nods. Short answers. One team member checked his watch. Another asked if we could "do this over Slack instead."

In the span of one week, I had taught six talented employees that meetings with me were a waste of their time.

WHAT I WAS ACTUALLY
DOING WRONG

For months, I thought the problem was context. In the interrogation room, the prison yard, the roadside stop, the purpose of the conversation was self-evident. Both parties knew why they were there. In business, I assumed the purpose would be equally obvious. But to Sarah, it wasn't.

That explanation is true. But it's incomplete.

It took me years, and a deep dive into the research on human motivation, to understand what I was really doing wrong. The insight didn't come from a management book. It came from Self-Determination Theory, the most rigorously tested framework in motivational psychology.

Here's what nobody told me in any of my many leadership or business roles: humans are driven by three core psychological needs. These aren't preferences or nice-to-haves. They're fundamental requirements for motivation, engagement, and well-being. Decades of research across cultures, industries, and contexts confirm this consistently:

- Autonomy: The need to feel in control of our own choices and actions. Not independence. Not isolation. Just the sense that we have a say in what happens to us.
- Competence: The need to feel capable and effective. To know that our work matters and that we're good at it.

- Relatedness: The need to feel connected to others. To be seen as a person, not a resource.

When these three needs are met, motivation flourishes naturally. We don't have to bribe people with bonuses or threaten them with performance reviews. They want to do good work because doing good work feels good.

When these needs are dismissed, people shut down. It doesn't matter how much we pay them, how impressive the title is, or how much they intellectually care about the mission. Block their psychological needs, and we block their motivation. It's not a choice they make. It's how humans work.

The challenge is that most organizations run on a completely different operating system (OS). Call it the Mechanical OS. It assumes that employees need to be closely managed and controlled. It values Compliance over Autonomy, Measurement over Competence, and Transaction over Relatedness. These aren't malicious choices. They're logical responses to real business pressures such as: risk management, accountability, and scalability. But the unintended consequence is a system that works against human nature.

"Organizations run on a Mechanical OS: Compliance, Control, and Transactions. Humans run on a different operating system entirely: Autonomy, Competence, and Relatedness. The mismatch is where motivation goes to die."

In that thirty-minute meeting with Sarah, I was running on the Mechanical OS. With the best of intentions, I managed to undermine all three of her psychological needs.

AUTONOMY

I controlled everything. I set the time. I wrote the agenda. I chose the questions. I directed the flow. Sarah had no ownership of the conversation. She was a passenger in a meeting that was supposedly "for her." Every time I glanced at my printed agenda, I signaled that her input was secondary to my plan.

COMPETENCE

My questions implied she might not be doing enough. "What's taking your bandwidth?" sounds neutral, but it carries an undertone of *prove to me you're busy*. I started with an audit, not with recognition of what she was doing well. Before she could feel competent, I made her feel evaluated.

RELATEDNESS

I treated her like a data source, not a human. Legal pad out, questions firing, and silence deployed as a tactic. She wasn't having a conversation with a colleague who cared about her. She was being interrogated by a stranger with a checklist.

Sarah's silence wasn't a sign of resistance. It wasn't

disengagement. It wasn't even shyness. It was the psychological shutdown response that happens when our core needs aren't being met. Her brain was doing exactly what it's designed to do: conserve energy and protect against threat when the environment signals that engagement won't be rewarded.

"Do we have to?" wasn't rudeness. It was a reasonable question: Why would I voluntarily return to an environment that makes me feel controlled, inadequate, and alone?

THE FRICTION WAS THE SIGNAL

Here's what I wish someone had told me that week: the friction I felt in those meetings wasn't a technique problem. It wasn't that I needed better questions or a different agenda template. The friction was a diagnostic signal.

Think of a one-on-one like the check engine light on your car's dashboard. When that light comes on, you have a choice. You can put tape over it and keep driving. You can get annoyed at the light for interrupting your day. Or you can recognize what it actually is: an early warning system telling you that something under the hood needs attention.

The light isn't the problem. The light is the signal. And if you ignore it long enough, what starts as a minor issue becomes an expensive breakdown on the side of the highway.

A one-on-one works the same way. When the meeting feels awkward, forced, or pointless, that's your check engine light. Something in the organizational system needs attention.

You can try to fix the meeting itself (tape over the light), get frustrated that employees aren't engaging (blame the light), or recognize the signal for what it is: an early warning that one or more psychological needs are being ignored.

If Sarah couldn't speak openly in a private meeting with her manager, what did that say about the team culture? If my instinct was to control and audit rather than listen and support, what did that say about how leadership was modeled throughout the organization? If the meeting felt transactional rather than human, was that pattern limited to this conference room, or did it run through everything?

It ran through everything. The Autonomy I stole was baked into our approval processes, our project management tools, and our performance review system. The Competence we undermined was embedded in our onboarding, feedback culture, and promotion criteria. The Relatedness we starved was built into our remote work policies, our team structures, and every efficiency initiative that prioritized output over connection.

The one-on-one didn't create these problems. It revealed them. And that's what makes it so valuable. We can hide a dysfunctional culture behind impressive dashboards and enthusiastic all-hands meetings. But we can't hide it in a thirty-minute conversation where one person asks one direct question after another, and the other person just sits there with nothing to say.

If this friction shows up in your one-on-ones, where else is it hiding?

This is how one-on-ones get "missed." Not always literally

skipped, though that happens too. But missed as a diagnostic opportunity. The meeting friction is data. It's telling us where our organization is accidentally working against human nature. Most leaders ignore the signal and try to fix the meeting. The better move is to read the signal and fix the system.

THE THREE WAYS
ONE-ON-ONES MISS

Let me define the term precisely. A "missed meeting" is any one-on-one that fails to support the three psychological needs. Whether it's literally skipped, poorly structured, or embedded in a culture that makes authentic conversation impossible.

The failure mode varies by level, but the underlying pattern is consistent:

- For entry-level managers, it's the skipped weekly session that lets small blockers fester into burnout. The need neglected: *Competence.* Employees feel stuck, unable to make progress, with no one helping them remove obstacles. They start to wonder if they're even capable of doing this job.

- For directors, it's the agenda-less check-in that devolves into venting without resolution. The need missed: *Autonomy.* Mid-level leaders feel like their concerns are heard but never acted on. They have a voice without real agency. They're consulted but not empowered.

- At the executive level, it's the surface-level monthly conversation that leaves everyone blindsided when things go wrong. The need unmet: *Relatedness.* There's no psychological safety for candor, so hard truths stay buried until they become expensive surprises.

Consider a CMO I knew who was fired after eight months of meetings she thought were positive. No one had told her that her metrics were off or that her communication style was alienating the board. Her one-on-ones with the CEO had been cordial and pleasant, but completely useless.

But here's the thing. The meetings weren't a failure. They were the check engine light.

What was likely happening is that the CEO was treating these sessions as status updates, a chance to share information and stay loosely aligned. The CMO, receiving no constructive feedback, reasonably interpreted the pleasant tone as approval. She wasn't missing signals. She was reading the signals she was given. The lack of candor created a hidden misalignment that blindsided two capable, proven leaders who simply weren't having the conversation they needed.

The same dynamic ran through the entire organization. Middle managers had learned not to escalate problems. Teams competed rather than collaborated. Success was performed rather than examined. This wasn't a CMO problem. It was a culture that had been quietly eroding for years, and now the rot had reached the executive floor. The CMO happened to be standing there when the floor gave way.

<table>
<tr><td>Low</td><td></td><td>High</td></tr>
<tr><td>The Transaction</td><td>The Sweet Spot</td><td></td></tr>
<tr><td>Void</td><td>The Black Hole</td><td></td></tr>
</table>

Y-axis: Follow Through. X-axis: Preparation Quality (Low to High).

THE MEETING FRICTION MAP

Here's a simple diagnostic framework. Think about your current one-on-ones and ask: where do they fall on this map, and what need might they be thwarting?

The map has two axes:

- Preparation Quality (Low to High): Do both parties arrive ready for a real conversation?

- Follow-Through (Low to High): Do commitments made in the meeting actually happen?

The four quadrants:

Low Prep, Low Follow-Through: "The Void" — Neither party prepares. Nothing gets done afterward. The meeting signals: your time doesn't matter. Employees stop bringing real concerns because nothing will happen anyway. Autonomy dies when their voice becomes pointless.

High Prep, Low Follow-Through: "The Black Hole" — Great agendas, thoughtful discussion, careful notes. Then nothing happens. Ideas die in the conference room. Employees start to feel like their input is collected but never valued. Why bother bringing your best thinking if it just disappears? Competence gets undermined when effort feels futile.

Low Prep, High Follow-Through: "The Transaction" — No structure, but things somehow get done. These meetings are all action, no connection. Efficient, maybe. But they feel transactional. There's no space for the human stuff: concerns, aspirations, the context that makes work meaningful. Relatedness starves when efficiency crowds out everything else.

High Prep, High Follow-Through: "The Sweet Spot" — Both parties arrive ready. Commitments get honored. There's structure and space for real conversation. These meetings support all three needs: employees have a voice (Autonomy), see their input matter (Competence), and feel genuinely seen (Relatedness).

Most organizations have meetings scattered across all four quadrants. The question isn't whether we have some bad meetings. The question is: what pattern do we see? And what does that pattern reveal about our culture?

THE COST OF WORKING AGAINST HUMAN NATURE

The organizational cost of missing these meetings is staggering. But not for the reasons most leadership books cite.

Gallup's research on millions of workers shows that employees with regular, meaningful one-on-ones are nearly three times more likely to be engaged at work. The typical interpretation then becomes: "One-on-ones are important. Do more of them."

But that conclusion misses the point entirely.

The companies spending millions on engagement initiatives (the pizza parties, the wellness apps, the motivational speakers) are getting three times worse results than companies that simply stopped dismissing their employees' psychological needs. We can't buy engagement with perks. We can stop inadvertently destroying it and address how humans actually function.

The one-on-one isn't a superficial engagement tactic we

tack onto a manager's schedule. It is a critical sensor for friction. A way to identify exactly where the organization is getting in its own way and what we need to stop doing.

That's not a soft metric. Engaged employees drive 21% higher profitability, show 37% lower absenteeism, and stay longer, effectively cutting the turnover costs that drain organizations. SHRM (Society for Human Resource Management) estimates replacing employee costs 50-200% of their annual salary. Do the math on your own turnover and watch the room get quiet.

The meeting isn't the cause. It's the check engine light.

When one-on-ones fail, they reveal a deeper pattern of systemic friction that is running through the organization. Fix the meeting without fixing the system, and you've just put tape over the dashboard. The engine is still failing. You just can't see the warning light anymore.

WHAT THIS BOOK WILL DO

This book will teach you how to run one-on-ones that support Autonomy, Competence, and Relatedness. You'll learn specific structures and frameworks that align with how humans actually work rather than fighting against it.

But more importantly, this book will teach you how to read the diagnostic signal.

Every chapter will ask: if this friction shows up in one-on-ones, where else is it hiding? Because the patterns that make meetings fail (the Autonomy blockers, the Competence traps, the Relatedness deficits) don't stay contained in a conference room. They run through hiring processes, performance management, leadership development, and entire cultures.

In the chapters ahead, we'll explore:

- The Psychology of the Mismatch: Why organizations run on a Mechanical OS while humans run on a completely different operating system, and what that mismatch costs every day

- Calibrating to Human Rhythms: How to stop letting the org chart dictate meeting frequency and start letting psychological needs be your guide

- Designing for Psychological Safety: Preparation that removes threat rather than adding bureaucracy

- The Needs-Support Framework: A feedback structure that fuels Competence and activates Autonomy (not another sandwich technique)

- Diagnosing Systemic Friction: When to recognize that the meeting problem is actually a system problem, and what to do about it

- What Your One-on-Ones Are Telling You: Expanding the lens from meeting optimization to organizational diagnosis

Each chapter includes practical frameworks you can implement this week. But more importantly, each chapter includes the diagnostic questions that reveal where the same patterns might be running through the rest of your organization.

The goal isn't to transform one-on-ones from "the meeting everyone dreads" into "the meeting that works." That's too small.

The goal is to use the one-on-one as the diagnostic tool it was always meant to be. To see where our organizations are accidentally working against human nature. And then to stop.

KEY TAKEAWAY:

One-on-ones don't fail because leaders lack technique. They fail because they're embedded in systems that inadvertently cripple Autonomy, Competence, and Relatedness.

CHAPTER TWO

THE COST OF GOOD INTENTIONS

What Systematic Need-Thwarting Actually Costs Your Organization

The previous chapter explained why one-on-ones fail: they inadvertently thwart Autonomy, Competence, and Relatedness. This chapter quantifies the damage.

But let me be clear about what we're measuring. The cost isn't "bad meetings." The cost is what happens when well-intentioned systems accidentally work against human nature. The meetings are just where the damage becomes visible.

Across U.S. businesses, poor workplace communication drains an estimated $1.2 trillion annually. That figure comes from Grammarly and Harris Poll research, and it accounts for lost productivity, preventable turnover, and the downstream effects of teams operating without alignment.

Most of us read that number and think: "We need better communication tools—more Slack channels. Clearer emails. Maybe a new project management system."

That's the logical response. It's also solving the wrong problem.

That $1.2 trillion isn't a communication problem. It's a psychological mismatch problem. It's what happens when organizations run on Compliance, Control, and Transaction while the humans inside them need Autonomy, Competence, and Relatedness. The miscommunication is a symptom. Unmet needs are the disease.

> "$1.2 trillion annually. That's not the cost of bad communication. That's the cost of well-intentioned systems working against human nature."

THE PATTERN NOBODY
SEES COMING

The pattern is predictable. Skip a few one-on-ones, and nothing visibly breaks. The team keeps shipping. Metrics hold steady. The meetings were optional all along. Or so it seems.

Then the cracks appear.

A top performer resigns, citing "lack of growth opportunities." Those opportunities were never discussed because the conversations never happened. Her Competence need went unfed for months. She found somewhere else that would feed it.

A project misses its deadline because a blocker sat unaddressed for six weeks. The engineer knew about it, but didn't feel safe raising it. His Relatedness need was so depleted that he'd stopped believing anyone cared about what he thought.

A problem explodes that three levels of management knew about, but the culture had taught them all the same lesson: surface a problem, own the blame. Executives never heard it coming because no one felt safe telling them. Middle managers kept quiet because they'd learned that raising concerns meant becoming responsible for fixing them. So everyone stayed silent, and the problem grew until it couldn't be ignored.

None of these outcomes came from malice. They came from good intentions operating inside systems that accidentally punish the behaviors we need most: honesty, initiative, and connection.

The data confirms what I've observed across finance, government, construction, and tech: the bill always comes due. The only question is when.

WHAT THE NUMBERS ACTUALLY MEAN

Let's break down that $1.2 trillion figure. It comes to approximately $12,500 per employee per year. That's money lost to unclear expectations, unaddressed blockers, and the friction of teams operating without shared understanding.

But here's what makes that number useful: it's a proxy for unmet human needs.

- Unclear expectations stifle Competence. How can any-one feel effective at their job when they don't know what success looks like?
- Unaddressed blockers impede Autonomy. We can see the obstacle. We might even know how to remove it. But we don't have the authority, the resources, or the support to act.
- Teams without shared understanding suffer from Relatedness deficits. They begin to feel there is no sense in working together because there is no apparent bene-fit. They are just individuals working in close proximity to one another, not with each other.

The one-on-one sits at the center of this problem. It's the primary mechanism for clarifying expectations (Competence), surfacing and removing blockers (Autonomy), and building genuine connection (Relatedness). When one-on-ones fail or don't happen, the $12,500 per employee starts accumulating.

But remember: the meeting is the check engine light, not the engine. Fix the meeting without fixing the system that made it fail, and we've just put tape over the dashboard.

CASE STUDY: THE $4 MILLION
CHECK ENGINE LIGHT

Numbers tell part of the story, patterns tell the rest. Let me share a case I observed firsthand. Details are altered for confidentiality, but the numbers are all too real.

INNOTECH: A RELATEDNESS
DEFICIT IN THE C-SUITE

A mid-sized tech company hired a CMO to lead their next growth phase. Impressive background, strong interview performance, and genuine strategic capability. For eight months, everything looked fine. Board meetings went smoothly. The CEO's informal check-ins were pleasant and high-level. Quarterly reviews showed reasonable progress.

What those check-ins lacked was candor.

The CEO never asked hard questions about pipeline metrics or competitive positioning. The CMO never surfaced concerns about resource constraints or timeline risks. Both assumed alignment because neither tested it.

This wasn't negligence. Both were busy, talented leaders doing their best with limited time. The CEO trusted the CMO's experience. The CMO trusted that she'd hear about problems if there were any. Each made reasonable assumptions that happened to be wrong.

In month nine, the CMO missed targets badly. The CEO,

blindsided, initiated her termination. The CMO was genuinely shocked. She'd received no indication that anything was wrong.

But the CMO's departure was only the first domino.

Without clear strategic direction from the top, the VP of Product and VP of Engineering had been operating on different assumptions. One was pivoting the roadmap toward enterprise clients. The other was optimizing for the existing base of medium-sized businesses. Neither knew they were misaligned because the executive team's one-on-ones had been surface-level status updates.

Q3 results reflected the chaos: revenue 23% below forecast, two key product launches delayed, and a 20% spike in voluntary turnover. Exit interviews cited "lack of direction" and "unclear priorities" repeatedly.

The result? Over $4 million lost. Failed CMO hire. Turnover. Missed revenue.

Were there other contributing factors? Almost certainly. But even a fraction of that loss was avoidable

So, what was the hidden problem?

I would argue that this wasn't a meeting problem. It was a Relatedness Deficit at the executive level. There was no psychological safety for honest conversation. The CEO's packed calendar and surface-level check-ins had inadvertently signaled that efficiency mattered more than connection. Hard truths felt risky to share. So nobody shared them.

The check engine light: Eight months of pleasant but useless one-on-ones. If anyone had been reading the signal, they would have noticed that no difficult topics ever surfaced. That's not harmony. That's fear wearing a professional mask.

Where else was it hiding? The same Relatedness Deficit that made executive meetings superficial ran through the entire culture. Middle managers had learned not to escalate problems. Teams had learned to compete rather than collaborate. The one-on-ones revealed what the org chart concealed: this was an organization where people worked near each other, not with each other.

KEY TAKEAWAY:

The $1.2 trillion annual cost of "poor communication" is really the cost of systematic need-stifling, all unintentional and usually driven by good intentions. Missed meetings don't just waste time. They create cascading failures that compound from individual frustration to team misalignment to organizational crisis. The InnoTech case shows the pattern: $4 million lost because pleasant, surface-level executive meetings made candor feel risky. The check engine light was on for eight months. Nobody was reading the signal. The damage is measurable. So is the fix. But the fix isn't better meetings.

CHAPTER THREE

THE PSYCHOLOGY OF ALIGNMENT

Why Needs-Supportive Meetings Change Behavior

hy do some one-on-ones work and others backfire? The answer lies in motivational psychology. Effective one-on-ones tap into how humans actually process feedback, build trust, and find meaning in their work. This isn't speculation. It's supported by decades of research from institutions including Harvard, Stanford, the National Institutes of Health, and Gallup's ongoing workplace studies.

My background in industrial-organizational psychology, combined with years of applying these principles in high-stakes environments, has shown me the same patterns repeatedly: when we understand the psychology, we run better meetings. When we ignore it, we trigger the exact responses we're trying to avoid.

The good news is that working with human psychology

isn't complicated. It simply requires mastering a few core principles that are often ignored in traditional training.

WHY RECOGNITION COMES FIRST

Let's start with how humans process feedback. When an employee receives genuine recognition for what they're doing well, something important happens psychologically: they feel capable. Their need for Competence gets fed.

This isn't just pleasant. It's functional. When people feel competent, they become more open to information, including insights into how they can improve. They associate the conversation with progress rather than threat. They're psychologically prepared for what comes next.

This is why sequence matters in feedback conversations. Lead with recognition, and you're working with how motivation actually works. Lead with criticism, and you're working against it.

The practical implication: opening a one-on-one with recognition (what I call "sustains") doesn't just feel pleasant. It creates the psychological conditions for receptivity. The employee experiences the meeting as a place where they're seen and valued, not just evaluated and found wanting.

"Recognition isn't the soft stuff before the real conversation. Recognition IS the real conversation. It creates the conditions where growth becomes possible."

THE TRUST FOUNDATION

The second psychological principle at play is trust. Paul Zak's research at Claremont Graduate University, widely covered in Harvard Business Review, measured trust in workplace settings and found something striking: high-trust environments correlate with 106% more energy at work, 76% higher engagement, and 50% greater productivity.

These aren't marginal gains. They're transformational. And they come from how people feel in their working relationships, not from new systems or better tools.

In Self-Determination Theory terms, trust is how Relatedness gets built. When we experience consistent, genuine attention from another person, when they follow through on commitments and show up predictably, we feel connected. That connection isn't just emotionally satisfying. It changes how we process everything else in the relationship.

One-on-ones are a primary mechanism for building this trust. When conducted well (with consistent scheduling, genuine attention, and follow-through on commitments), they create the conditions for deep Relatedness. When conducted poorly (distracted manager, broken commitments, unpredictable cancellations), they do the opposite.

Here's the diagnostic question: if trust is low in your one-on-ones, where else is it low? Trust doesn't exist in isolation. The same patterns that erode trust in a thirty-minute meeting (inconsistency, broken commitments, distracted attention) are probably showing up in team dynamics, in cross-functional relationships, and in how leadership communicates with the organization. The one-on-one is just where we notice it first.

WHY CRITICISM TRIGGERS SHUTDOWN

Research from the NeuroLeadership Institute, highlighted in PwC's strategy+business, found that heart rates can spike up to 50% during feedback conversations. That's a stress response comparable to public speaking.

Why does feedback trigger such an intense response? Because criticism, especially from someone with power over our career, registers as a social threat. And humans respond to social threat the same way we respond to physical threat: we protect ourselves.

When employees feel threatened, openness decreases. Receptivity to new information drops. They may nod along, but they're not processing. They're protecting. The meeting becomes something to survive rather than something to learn from.

This is why so many well-intentioned feedback conversations fail. The manager delivers carefully prepared criticism. The employee appears to receive it. Nothing changes. The manager concludes the employee "doesn't want to grow" or "can't take feedback." But the real problem was that the conversation triggered a threat response that made genuine reception impossible.

The research also shows that this response can be modulated. When feedback conversations begin with recognition, and when growth areas are framed as forward-looking opportunities rather than past failures, the stress response diminishes. The employee shifts from defense to collaboration.

This is why the "sustains before improves" structure isn't just nice. It's strategic. We're sequencing the conversation to work with human psychology rather than against it.

"The employee who 'can't take feedback' often can. They just can't take feedback delivered in a way that triggers their threat response."

KEY TAKEAWAY:

Effective one-on-ones work because they satisfy core psychological needs: recognition feeds Competence, consistency builds Relatedness, and purposeful connection activates Autonomy. The research is clear: recognition before criticism, future-focused feedback, and explicit connection to mission create the conditions for engagement and growth. The same principles that make meetings work are the principles that make organizations work. Master them in the one-on-one, then ask where else they need to be applied.

CHAPTER FOUR

THE SUSTAIN-IMPROVE FRAMEWORK

*A Structure for Feedback
That Actually Lands*

The previous chapter explained the psychology behind effective one-on-ones. This chapter gives you the core methodology for applying it.

The Sustain-Improve Framework is a practical structure for delivering feedback that feeds psychological needs rather than ignoring them. It's not complicated. But it's precise. And precision matters when we're working with human psychology.

THE STRUCTURE

Every feedback conversation follows the same pattern:

- Three Sustains: Specific things the employee is doing well that should continue. These feed Competence.
- Three Improves: Specific areas for growth, framed as forward-looking process improvements. These activate Autonomy by inviting the employee into problem-solving.
- Co-Creation: After presenting Improves, invite the employee to propose solutions. This shifts from evaluation to collaboration.

The sequence is intentional. Sustains come first because recognition creates the psychological conditions for receptivity. Improves come second because the employee is now primed to hear growth areas as opportunities rather than threats. Co-creation comes last because the employee owns the solution rather than having it imposed.

WHAT MAKES A GOOD SUSTAIN

A sustain is not "good job." A Sustain is specific, observable, and connected to impact.

Bad Sustain: "You're doing great work."

Good Sustain: "The documentation you wrote for the API integration was exceptionally clear. The new developer was able to get onboarded two days faster because of it."

The difference is precision. Generic praise feels hollow. Specific recognition lands. When we can name exactly what someone did well and connect it to concrete outcomes, we're feeding their Competence need with substance rather than empty calories.

Three sustains per meeting forces us to pay attention. We can't deliver three specific observations unless we've actually been watching. That attention itself is a form of Relatedness.

WHAT MAKES A GOOD IMPROVE

An Improve is not "you need to do better." An Improve is future-focused, process-oriented, and specific.

Bad Improve: "You've been missing deadlines."

Good Improve: "Let's talk about how to build in more buffer time on the next project. One thing that might help is flagging potential blockers earlier in the week so we can address them before they compound."

The difference is framing. Past-focused criticism triggers defense. Past-focused criticism triggers defense. Future-focused feedback activates problem-solving. Same underlying issue. Completely different psychological response.

Three Improves per meeting prevents both extremes. Fewer than three and we're probably avoiding difficult truths. More than three, and we're overwhelming the employee, triggering the threat response we're trying to avoid.

THE CO-CREATION MOMENT

After presenting improves, pause and invite collaboration: "What do you think? What steps could address this? How can I support you?"

This is the moment where Autonomy gets fed. The employee isn't receiving a verdict. They're participating in their own development. The solutions that emerge are ones they've helped create, which means they're far more likely to actually implement them.

Co-creation also surfaces information we might not have. The employee often knows context we don't. When we invite their perspective rather than dictating solutions, we frequently discover that the "problem" looked different from their vantage point, or that they have ideas we hadn't considered.

"The manager who dictates solutions gets compliance. The manager who co-creates solutions gets commitment."

KEY TAKEAWAY:

The Sustain-Improve Framework structures feedback to work with psychology rather than against it. Three specific sustains feed Competence and create receptivity, while three future-focused Improves activate Autonomy through problem-solving. Co-creation ensures the employee owns the solution. The sequence matters: recognition first, growth areas second, collaboration third. This isn't a template for making feedback feel nice. It's a precision tool for making feedback land.

CHAPTER FIVE

CALIBRATING THE CADENCE

Matching Meeting Rhythm to Psychological Needs

The previous chapter provided the core feedback methodology. This chapter addresses when to meet and how often. The right cadence isn't a universal formula. It depends on the role, the context, and the specific psychological needs most likely to go unmet. Here are some guidelines for calibrating one-on-one frequency across organizational levels.

INDIVIDUAL CONTRIBUTORS: WEEKLY, 30 MINUTES

For individual contributors, weekly thirty-minute sessions work best. This cadence catches blockers early, provides regular feedback cycles, and maintains a consistent connection.

The psychological logic: individual contributors often face the highest risk of Competence-challenges. They're doing detailed work where small blockers can compound into big frustrations. Without regular touchpoints, they may struggle in silence, wondering if they're capable of doing the job. Weekly check-ins provide the setting to surface and address these blockers before they become competence problems.

Weekly check-ins also feed Relatedness. For team members who might otherwise feel like cogs in a machine, a protected thirty minutes signals: "You matter enough for dedicated time."

MANAGERS: BI-WEEKLY, 45 MINUTES

For managers, bi-weekly sessions of approximately forty-five minutes provide enough space for strategic conversation without creating meeting overload.

The psychological logic: Managers need more Autonomy than individual contributors. They're making decisions, leading teams, shaping outcomes. Weekly check-ins can feel like micromanagement. Bi-weekly respects their need for space while maintaining alignment.

The longer format (45 vs. 30 minutes) acknowledges that manager-level conversations cover more ground: their own development, their team's dynamics, cross-functional challenges, and strategic questions that require more than tactical answers.

EXECUTIVES: MONTHLY OR QUARTERLY, 60 MINUTES

For C-suite executives, shift to monthly or quarterly meetings of approximately 60 minutes.

The rationale: Executives operate at a strategic altitude. Their decisions have longer time horizons. Their calendars are at capacity, making weekly tactical check-ins would be a poor use of their time and yours. But the absence of structured conversations creates the conditions for the kind of blindsiding scenario described in Chapter 2: the CMO fired after months of "positive" meetings where no one surfaced real concerns.

A monthly or quarterly cadence acknowledges their time constraints while ensuring meaningful connection doesn't disappear entirely. The longer format (60 minutes) allows for the kind of honest, candid conversation that can't be rushed.

WHEN TO ADJUST

These recommendations are starting points, not rigid rules. The cadence should respond to your observations, instead of following a rigid formula.

Scale back temporarily when alignment is strong. After a project wraps smoothly or during stable periods, reducing frequency can prevent meeting fatigue. But maintain at least quarterly touchpoints to preserve the Relatedness foundation.

Scale up during transitions, such as a new role, a new project, or an organizational change. These moments require more frequent check-ins until stability returns. Transitions are when an employee's human needs are most often ignored.

Watch for signals of misalignment. If employees seem disengaged, if the same issues resurface repeatedly, if surprises keep emerging, the cadence may be too infrequent. Conversely, if meetings feel hollow and employees seem to dread them, the cadence may be too frequent.

KEY TAKEAWAY:

Match cadence to role: weekly for individual contributors, biweekly for managers, monthly or quarterly for executives. But understand why: predictable rhythm feeds Relatedness, frequent touchpoints catch Competence-stifling early, and appropriate spacing respects Autonomy. The specific numbers matter less than the underlying principle: match the frequency to where each role is most likely to experience need deficits, then adjust based on what you observe.

CHAPTER SIX

PREPARATION

*How to Remove the Threat Before
the Meeting Starts*

The previous chapter established cadence. This chapter addresses what happens before the meeting starts.

Preparation is the difference between a one-on-one that creates value and one that wastes time. Show up without structure, and you get blank stares and reluctant participation. Show up with a shared agenda and clear purpose, and the dynamic shifts entirely.

But here's the insight most preparation advice misses: the primary purpose of preparation isn't efficiency. It's threat removal.

When employees don't know what's coming in a meeting with their manager, they arrive in a defensive posture. What does she want to talk about? Am I in trouble? Is this about that thing from last week? The ambiguity itself triggers the threat response we discussed in Chapter 3. Before a word is spoken, the employee is already protecting rather than engaging.

Good preparation eliminates that ambiguity. It tells the employee: here's what we'll discuss, here's what I'd like you to think about, here's the space for your concerns. The meeting becomes predictable in the best sense. The threat dissolves before either person enters the room.

"The primary purpose of preparation isn't efficiency. It's threat removal. Ambiguity triggers defense. Clarity creates safety."

WHY PREPARATION MATTERS PSYCHOLOGICALLY

Preparation shifts the meeting's psychological frame in three ways, each mapping to the core needs:

- It feeds Autonomy. When employees receive an agenda in advance, they have time to prepare their own thoughts. They arrive with agency rather than reactivity. The meeting becomes something they participate in, not something done to them.
- It protects Competence. Advance notice prevents the ambush that makes people feel stupid. "I don't know" is embarrassing when you're caught off guard. It's

reasonable when you've been given time to think and genuinely don't have the answer yet.

- It builds Relatedness. A shared agenda signals: "I respect your time enough to prepare. I expect you to do the same. We're partners in this conversation." That's a fundamentally different dynamic than "let me see what's on my mind when we sit down."

THE AGENDA TEMPLATE

Share the agenda at least 24 hours before the meeting. This gives both parties time to reflect and arrive prepared.

- Section 1: Employee-Led Opening (10 minutes) — They walk through their prepared items: wins, blockers, concerns. Their agenda, not yours. Example: "I want to talk about the client escalation I handled, a resource constraint on the migration project, and my timeline for the certification." *Psychological function: Feeds Autonomy.*
- Section 2: Alignment Check (5 minutes) — Connect their work to team objectives. Review progress on action items from last meeting. Example: "How does the migration project tie into our Q2 priorities? And where are we on the vendor outreach you committed to last week?" *Psychological function: Feeds Competence.*
- Section 3: Feedback & Development (10 minutes) — Three sustains, three improves, co-create solutions.

Example: "Your client communication has been excellent. One area to work on: tightening up your status updates so the team can plan around dependencies. What would help you do that?" *Psychological function: Sustains feed Competence, co-creation feeds Autonomy.*

- Section 4: Action Items & Close (5 minutes) — Summarize commitments with owners and deadlines. Ask: "Anything we didn't cover?" Confirm a time for the next meeting. Example: "You'll send me the revised timeline by Thursday. I'll follow up with finance by Monday. Anything else before we wrap?" *Psychological function: Follow-through builds Relatedness.*

The sequence is intentional. Starting with employee concerns immediately encourage Autonomy. The meeting is theirs. Not an obligation to endure. Not an evaluation to survive. Not a status report to deliver. Theirs. That shift in ownership changes everything about how they show up.

COMMON PITFALLS

- No agenda at all. Arriving without structure signals that the meeting isn't important enough to prepare for. The deeper damage is psychological: no agenda means maximum ambiguity, which means maximum threat response.

- Last-minute agenda dumps. Sending the agenda an hour before the meeting defeats the purpose. The employee has no time to reflect.
- Overloaded agendas. Cramming too many topics into one meeting leads to rushed conversations. Chronic overload teaches employees that the meeting will always feel frantic.
- Manager-centric framing. If every agenda item is something you want to discuss, the employee experiences the meeting as a status report rather than a dynamic conversation.

KEY TAKEAWAY:

Share the agenda 24 hours ahead. Start with employee concerns, not yours. Include prep questions that invite reflection. Review past notes for continuity. But understand why: the purpose of preparation isn't efficiency. It's threat removal. Ambiguity triggers the defensive response that shuts down receptivity. Clarity signals safety and respect. The meeting's value is largely determined before it begins.

RUNNING THE MEETING

From Opening to Action Items

This chapter covers execution: what happens during the meeting itself.

The goal isn't to dominate the conversation. It's to guide it. Your job in the moment is to create space for genuine dialogue while ensuring all three psychological needs are met.

You've got the structure. Now let's talk about what to actually do and say.

THE FRAMEWORK SERVES THE PERSON

A quick word before we dive in: the structure exists to serve the person, not the other way around.

If an employee walks in visibly upset about something that just happened, you don't say, "That's not on the agenda." If a breakthrough conversation is happening in the alignment check, you don't cut it off because it's time for feedback. If they need the whole meeting to work through one blocker, then that's the meeting.

The framework is the scaffolding. It gives shape to the conversation so both parties know what to expect. But the moment the framework gets in the way of the person, abandon it.

Rigid adherence to structure is just another form of Autonomy-denial. The goal is never to run a perfect meeting. The goal is to feed psychological needs. Sometimes that means following the template. Sometimes that means throwing it out.

Read the room. Serve the person. Now let's dive back into it.

OPENING THE CONVERSATION

They prepared. You prepared. Now what?

Don't start with small talk that drags on. Don't start with your agenda. Start by handing them the floor: "You had some things you wanted to cover. Let's start there."

Then do something hard: stay quiet.

"Resist the urge to fill silence. If they pause, wait. Silence often precedes the most important thing someone has to say. If we jump in to rescue them from the pause, we signal their reflection isn't worth the wait. That's undermining Autonomy disguised as helpfulness."

Google's Project Aristotle study, which analyzed over 180 teams, found that psychological safety was the single strongest predictor of team success. One-on-ones are a primary mechanism for building it. But only if the employee actually gets to speak.

LISTENING FOR WHAT'S NOT BEING SAID

The words are only part of the conversation. Pay attention to:

- What they avoid. If they consistently steer away from certain projects or people, that's data.
- How they describe blockers. "It's fine" with a flat tone isn't fine.
- Energy shifts. When do they lean in? When do they pull back?
- What they ask about. Questions reveal concerns they're not stating directly.

In remote meetings, this is harder. Use video. Nonverbal cues are essential for reading how the conversation is landing. Audio-only meetings lose too much information.

THE ALIGNMENT CHECK

Transition with something like: "Let's talk about how your work is connecting to our broader goals."

This section serves two purposes: it ensures the employee sees their work as meaningful, and it surfaces misalignment early.

Review action items from the previous meeting. What was committed? What was completed? What got blocked? This creates accountability and shows that you're tracking their trajectory over time. That continuity feeds Relatedness: "You remember. You're paying attention. I matter beyond this single meeting."

If there's a gap between what they're working on and what the team needs, this is where you catch it. Don't let misalignment fester for weeks.

DELIVERING FEEDBACK
THAT LANDS

You've built safety through the opening. You've connected their work to purpose. Now comes feedback.

Start with sustains. Three specific things they're doing well. Not vague praise. Concrete recognition: "The way you handled the client escalation last week showed real composure. The documentation you produced on the new system is being used as a model by other teams."

This isn't softness. It's strategy. Recognition feeds Competence and creates receptivity. An employee who feels seen and valued is psychologically more open to hearing where they can grow. Skip the sustains, and you're working against how humans process feedback.

Then Improves. Three areas for growth, framed as process improvements rather than personal criticism. Future-focused, not past-focused. "One thing that would help the team: getting status updates out earlier so others can plan around dependencies" lands differently than "You're always late with your updates."

Then co-create. After presenting improves, ask: "What do you think? What steps could address this? How can I support you?" This shifts the dynamic from evaluation to collaboration. They own the solution rather than having it imposed.

MANAGING AIRTIME

Aim for roughly 70% employee talk, 30% manager talk.

If you're doing most of the talking, you're not learning anything. The employee isn't processing. They're just receiving. That's not a conversation. It's a lecture with a captive audience.

Check yourself mid-meeting. Who's been talking more? If it's you, ask a question and stay quiet.

STAYING ON TRACK

Tangents feel productive in the moment, but often lead to important items being rushed or dropped.

If something significant comes up that's off-agenda, acknowledge it: "That's important. Let's put it on the agenda for next time so we can give it the attention it deserves." Then return to the structure.

Chronic tangent-chasing teaches employees that the meeting has no real shape. That undermines the safety that the structure provides.

HANDLING DIFFICULT MOMENTS

Sometimes feedback lands badly. The employee gets defensive, shuts down, or pushes back hard.

Don't escalate. Don't retreat. Stay curious.

"I'm sensing this feedback isn't landing the way I intended. Help me understand your perspective."

The goal isn't to win the moment. It's to keep the conversation open. Defensiveness is a signal that a need is being stifled. Usually Competence. Sometimes Autonomy. Back up, acknowledge their perspective, and try a different angle.

If the conversation gets stuck, it's okay to pause: "Let's both think about this and revisit it next time." Not every issue gets resolved in one meeting.

CLOSING WITH CLARITY

Never end a one-on-one without clear commitments.

Summarize what each person will do. Be specific: who, what, by when. "You'll send the revised timeline by Thursday. I'll follow up with finance by Monday."

Then ask: "Anything we didn't cover?"

This matters. Sometimes, the most important thing they needed to say was waiting for permission. Give them one last opening before you close.

Preview the next meeting: "Anything you want to make sure we cover next time?" This creates continuity and gives them ownership of the ongoing agenda.

THE CUMULATIVE EFFECT

One good meeting doesn't change much. A pattern of good meetings changes everything.

Each conversation builds on the last. Trust compounds. Employees start bringing real concerns because they've learned those concerns get heard. Feedback lands because it comes from someone who sees their strengths, not just their gaps. Action items stick because both parties know they'll be reviewed.

The meeting becomes a resource they use, not an obligation they endure.

The goal is not to have a perfect meeting. Rather, it's having a meeting that consistently feeds psychological needs, so people start showing up differently.

KEY TAKEAWAY:

Execution is about presence, not performance. Listen more than you talk. Watch for what's not being said. Deliver sustains before improves. Co-create solutions rather than dictating them. Close with clear commitments. The structure is there to support, not to supersede the individual's needs. Your job is to give that person's needs genuine attention. Do that consistently, and the meetings start working for both of you.

CHAPTER EIGHT

FOLLOW-UP STRATEGY

*How Trust Gets Built (or Broken)
After the Meeting Ends*

A good one-on-one can surface important insights, remove blockers, and build genuine connection. But without follow-up, progress evaporates. Action items drift. Commitments fade. By the next meeting, you're starting from scratch.

Follow-up is where conversations become results. It's the difference between meetings that just feel productive in the moment and meetings that actually move the needle.

But here's the deeper insight: follow-up is where Relatedness gets built or broken. Every commitment we make in a one-on-one is a small promise. When we keep those promises, trust deepens. When we don't, it erodes. The meeting itself might feed all three psychological needs perfectly. However, if there's no follow-through, Relatedness takes the hit.

> "Every commitment in a one-on-one is a small promise. Keep enough of them, and trust compounds. Break enough of them, and the meeting itself stops mattering."

WHY FOLLOW-UP GETS SKIPPED

It feels like admin work. We had the conversation. We covered the topics. Moving on to the next thing feels more productive than documenting what just happened.

But research consistently shows that insights without reinforcement don't stick. Most feedback goes unimplemented, not because people reject it, but because the daily grind pushes it out of focus. A week later, the specifics blur. A month later, the conversation might as well not have happened.

Follow-up creates the accountability loop that turns intentions into action. It's not paperwork. It's the mechanism that makes the meeting matter.

And psychologically, skipping follow-up sends a signal: "What we discussed wasn't important enough to remember. Your concerns weren't significant enough to track. The commitments I made weren't real commitments." That's thwarting Relatedness, even if we don't intend it that way.

THE PSYCHOLOGICAL FUNCTION OF FOLLOW-UP

- Relatedness: Trust is built through commitments kept over time. Follow-up is the visible evidence that we're tracking, remembering, and following through. It says: "You matter enough that I wrote this down. Our conversation was real."

- Competence: Progress tracking transforms visibility into growth. When employees can see their development arc over time, they can feel their competence needs being met. They're not just completing tasks. They're becoming more capable, and they can see it.

- Autonomy: Documentation creates shared ownership. When both parties can see the commitments and track progress together, the dynamic becomes collaborative rather than supervisory. The employee isn't being monitored. They're participating in their own accountability.

THE 24-HOUR RULE

Send a recap within 24 hours. Not a transcript. A brief summary that captures:

- What was discussed. The key topics, concerns raised, and decisions made. This creates a shared record that both parties can reference.

- What each person committed to. Specific action items with owners and deadlines. "You'll draft the proposal by Friday. I'll connect you with the finance team by Wednesday." Notice that both parties have commitments. This isn't a manager assigning tasks. It's mutual accountability.
- What's next. Agenda items for the following meeting. This creates continuity and signals that progress will be tracked. It also gives the employee input into what's coming, feeding Autonomy.

Keep it short. A few bullet points in an email or a quick update to a shared doc. The goal is clarity, not completeness. Lengthy recaps become a burden that leads to abandonment.

Why 24 hours? Because memory fades fast. The details that seem vivid right after the meeting become hazy within days. And psychologically, prompt follow-up signals priority. A recap that arrives a week later says: "I finally got around to this." A recap within 24 hours says, "This mattered enough to do immediately."

TRACK PROGRESS, NOT JUST TASKS

Action items are binary: done or not done. Progress tracking goes deeper.

In each follow-up, reference what was working (sustains) and what was being developed (improves) from previous conversations. Start the next meeting with: "Last time we talked about improving your cross-team communication. How's that going?"

This creates a running narrative. People can see their own development over time. They're not just completing tasks. They're growing. That visibility matters enormously for Competence. It's the difference between feeling like you're on a treadmill (endless tasks, no progress) and feeling like you're on a journey (clear development arc, measurable growth).

Keep a simple log. A shared doc works. So does a notes app. The format matters less than the habit of referencing it. When we open a one-on-one by reviewing the previous conversation's themes and commitments, we're communicating: "I remember. This is continuous. Your development matters beyond any single meeting."

"Progress tracking transforms the feeling from 'endless tasks, no progress' to 'clear development arc, measurable growth.' That visibility feeds Competence directly."

THE COMPOUNDING EFFECT

Follow-up has a compounding quality. Each documented conversation builds on the last. Patterns emerge. Progress becomes visible. Trust deepens because people see that what they say actually matters and that it's tracked.

The first few follow-ups might feel mechanical. But over months, a different dynamic will emerge. The employee starts referencing past conversations unprompted: "Remember when we talked about my presentation skills? I think that's improved, but I'm still struggling with the Q&A portion." They've internalized the developmental frame. They're tracking their own growth.

That's Competence growth at scale. The employee isn't just receiving feedback. They're actively engaged in their own development. The one-on-one has become a resource they use, not an obligation they endure.

For remote and hybrid teams, this compounding effect matters even more. Without the informal check-ins that happen naturally in offices, the formal one-on-one carries more weight.

TOOLS THAT WORK

Keep it simple. The best follow-up system is the one you'll actually use.

- For individuals: A shared Google Doc or OneNote notebook works well. One running document per direct report, updated after each meeting. Easy to reference, easy to search. The running document becomes a visible record of the relationship over time.

- For teams: Slack or Teams channels can house quick recaps. Tag action items so they're searchable. Link to the central doc for longer notes.
- For larger organizations: Tools like Asana, Notion, or your HR system can formalize the tracking. Action items auto-sync with calendars. Notes feed into performance reviews.

The trap is over-engineering. If the system creates more work than it saves, people abandon it. Start with the simplest tool that captures the essentials. Add complexity only if you genuinely need it.

The goal is sustainability. A perfect system that gets abandoned after three weeks does less good than an imperfect system that persists for years. Choose friction-free over feature-rich.

THE DIAGNOSTIC QUESTION

Here's the question to ask after implementing follow-up practices: where else do commitments get made and forgotten in our organization?

If skipped follow-up erodes Relatedness in one-on-ones, the same pattern likely runs through broader organizational communication. How often do all-hands meetings end with announced initiatives that never get referenced again? How often do strategic priorities get declared and then quietly abandoned? How often do executives make commitments that everyone knows won't be kept?

Each of these is a follow-up failure at the organizational scale. And each one erodes trust the same way a skipped one-on-one follow-up does. The message is consistent: "What we say doesn't actually matter. Commitments aren't real. Words are just words."

If follow-up builds trust in one-on-ones, what would follow-up look like for organizational commitments? Regular progress updates on announced initiatives. Explicit acknowledgment when priorities shift. Honest communication when something promised doesn't happen. The principle is the same: kept commitments build trust, and broken commitments erode it.

"How often do all-hands announcements never get referenced again? How often do strategic priorities quietly disappear? Each is a follow-up failure that erodes trust at scale."

THE FIVE-MINUTE HABIT

Without follow-up, even great conversations fade. With it, each meeting builds on the last.

The habit takes five minutes. Immediately after the meeting (or within 24 hours), capture the key points: what was discussed, what was committed to, what's next. Send it or update the shared doc. Done.

Five minutes per meeting. The impact compounds for months. Trust builds conversation by conversation. Competence becomes visible over time. Relatedness deepens through kept commitments.

It's not glamorous work. But it's the work that makes everything else stick. The meeting might be where insights surface. Follow-up is where they become reality.

KEY TAKEAWAY:

Send a recap within 24 hours: what was discussed, what each person committed to, what's next. Track progress over time, not just task completion. Use the simplest tool that works. But understand why: follow-up is where Relatedness gets built. Every kept commitment deepens trust. Every forgotten commitment erodes it. The habit takes five minutes. The impact compounds for months. And the same principle applies beyond one-on-ones: wherever commitments get made and forgotten in your organization, trust is degrading. Follow-up is the antidote.

WHEN THE MEETING ISN'T THE PROBLEM

Reading the Organizational Signal

You've got the structure. The sustain-improve feedback. Employee-led openings. Shared agendas sent 24 hours ahead. Cadences are matched to the role. Follow up within a day. You're doing the work.

But sometimes it still doesn't work.

Despite solid prep and smooth execution, some one-on-ones just don't click. The same issues resurface. Engagement stays flat. Both parties dread the calendar invite. When this happens, the instinct is to try harder: more prep, more structure, more frequency.

But here's what this book has been building toward: when good technique still produces bad meetings, the meeting isn't the problem.

The meeting is the check engine light. And if the light keeps flashing despite your best maintenance, it's time to look under the hood.

"When good technique still produces bad meetings, the meeting isn't the problem. It's a signal. The question is: what is it signaling?"

THE MEETING AS AN ORGANIZATIONAL DIAGNOSTIC

Throughout this book, we've asked "Where else?" after each practice. Where else does ambiguity create a threat? Where else do commitments get forgotten? Where else does the sequence of conversation matter?

Those questions weren't just about extending meeting techniques to other contexts. They were diagnostic questions. Because the patterns that show up in one-on-ones rarely exist in isolation. They're symptoms of broader organizational dynamics.

When a one-on-one fails despite good technique, it's usually because the meeting is trying to solve a problem that exists outside the meeting. The employee's Autonomy isn't being undermined by how you run the conversation. It's being undermined by how the organization runs everything else. The meeting can't fix that. But it can reveal it.

RED FLAGS AND WHAT
THEY SIGNAL

Here are several patterns that indicate the problem is bigger than the meeting, along with what they typically reveal about the organization:

1. Pattern: Pure Venting Without Traction

What it looks like: The meeting becomes a complaint session. Problems surface repeatedly, but solutions never emerge or stick. Energy drains. Nothing improves. The employee seems relieved to have voiced concerns, but nothing changes as a result.

What it signals organizationally: The employee has learned that raising concerns doesn't lead to change. This is usually a symptom of broader Autonomy-thwarting: decisions are made elsewhere, input is ignored, or there's no mechanism for bottom-up influence. The venting isn't a meeting problem. It's the only outlet available in a system that doesn't listen.

Where else to look: How does the organization handle feedback generally? When employees raise concerns in other forums, what happens? Is there a pattern of the organization soliciting input and then ignoring it?

2. Pattern: Recurring Blockers That Never Clear

What it looks like: Despite co-created action items, the same issues appear week after week. The blockers get discussed, plans get made, and then nothing changes. The employee seems frustrated but resigned.

What it signals organizationally: The blockers probably aren't within the employee's control to solve, or within yours. This is often a symptom of systemic friction: broken processes, missing resources, or dependencies on other teams that aren't responsive. The one-on-one surfaces the blocker, but the organization doesn't have a mechanism to clear it.

Where else to look: Are the same blockers showing up across multiple employees? Across multiple teams? If so, the problem isn't individual performance. It's organizational infrastructure.

3. Pattern: Consistent Dread Despite Good Structure

What it looks like: Repeated reschedules. Minimal input when meetings do happen. Body language that screams "get me out of here." One blank-stare-meeting is normal. A pattern indicates something deeper.

What it signals organizationally: The employee may have learned that vulnerability is punished, that honesty backfires, or that these conversations are actually surveillance disguised as support. This is often a symptom of a broader trust deficit: past experiences (with you or previous managers) have taught them that one-on-ones are unsafe. The meeting technique can't overcome organizational memory.

Where else to look: What's the history here? Has candor been punished before? Has feedback been weaponized? Is there organizational trauma that makes openness feel risky?

4. Pattern: Sustains Land, Improves Don't

What it looks like: The employee responds well to recognition but shuts down or deflects when growth areas come up. Feedback conversations feel one-sided. Development stalls.

What it signals organizationally: The employee may have learned that "areas for improvement" is code for "reasons you might get fired." This is often a symptom of a fear-based performance culture: feedback has been used punitively, improvement areas have been held against people, or the organization conflates development with deficiency. The employee isn't resistant to growth. They're protecting themselves.

Where else to look: How does the organization handle performance reviews? Is feedback separated from compensation and promotion decisions? Is development treated as investment or as remediation?

5. Pattern: Disengagement Despite Apparent Alignment

What it looks like: The meetings seem fine. Structure is followed. Action items get completed. But energy is low. There's no spark. The employee is going through the motions.

What it signals organizationally: The employee may be experiencing a broader deficit in meaning. They're not struggling with the work or with you. They're struggling to see why any of it matters. This is often a symptom of purpose disconnection at scale: the organization hasn't made the mission real, the work feels like cogs in a machine, or there's a gap between stated values and lived experience.

Where else to look: How does the organization communicate purpose? Is there a clear line between individual work and organizational mission? Or is "purpose" just something on a poster in the lobby?

THE LIMITS OF MEETING TECHNIQUE

Here's the honest truth: a well-run one-on-one can't fix a broken organization.

It can create a pocket of safety in an unsafe culture. It can provide temporary relief from chronic need deficits. It can help an individual employee feel seen, even when the broader system doesn't. These are valuable outcomes.

But if the organization is systematically undermining

Autonomy through micromanagement and approval bottlenecks, a 30-minute meeting can't overcome the other 39.5 hours of the week. If the organization is systematically eroding Competence through broken tools and impossible expectations, one conversation won't restore the sense of mastery. If the organization is systematically starving Relatedness through isolation and competition, a single human connection can't fill the void.

The one-on-one is powerful. But it's not magic. When organizational dysfunction is severe enough, the meeting becomes a pressure relief valve at best, a place to vent before returning to the same broken environment.

> "A well-run one-on-one can create a pocket of safety in an unsafe culture. But it can't fix the culture. If the broader system is working against basic human needs, the meeting becomes a pressure relief valve, not a solution."

WHAT TO DO WHEN IT'S SYSTEMIC

If the patterns above look familiar, if multiple employees show the same signs, if good technique consistently produces disappointing results, then the intervention needed isn't at the meeting level. It's at the organizational level.

First, name what you're seeing. Whether you're noticing it in your own one-on-ones or hearing it from your managers, put language to it: 'Blockers keep recurring despite our action plans. I don't think the problem is in how we're running these meetings. I think there's something systemic we're bumping into.

Second, look for patterns across conversations. If multiple employees are showing the same signals, that's confirmation. One person's venting might be an individual issue. Five people's venting is an organizational one.

Third, escalate the pattern, not just the symptom. Don't go to leadership saying, "Sarah seems disengaged." Go saying "I'm seeing a pattern across my team that suggests our approval processes are creating frustration that individual conversations can't resolve. Here's what I'm observing, and here's what I think it indicates about our broader systems."

Fourth, recognize what's in your control and what isn't. You can run excellent one-on-ones. You can name systemic patterns. You can escalate with clarity. You may not be able to fix organizational dysfunction by yourself. That's not failure. That's acknowledging the scope of the problem.

THE BIGGER PICTURE

This book started with a simple premise: one-on-ones matter, and most of us aren't doing them well. The chapters that followed gave you the tools to do them better.

But the deeper premise has been building throughout: the one-on-one is a window into organizational health. When meetings work, it's usually because the broader environment supports the psychological needs we've been discussing. When meetings fail despite good technique, it's usually because the broader environment is thwarting those needs at scale.

The "Where else?" questions throughout this book weren't tangents. They were pointing toward this conclusion: the patterns that make meetings work or fail are the same patterns that make organizations work or fail. Autonomy, Competence, Relatedness. These aren't meeting concepts. They're human concepts. And they operate at every level of organizational life.

If your one-on-ones are struggling, start with technique. The practices in this book will help. But if technique isn't enough, don't assume you're doing something wrong. Ask what the meeting is revealing about the broader system. Use it as the diagnostic tool that it's designed to be.

"The check engine light is on. Don't put tape over the dashboard. Look under the hood."

PRACTICAL ADJUSTMENTS WHILE YOU WORK ON THE BIGGER ISSUES

While systemic issues are being addressed (or while you're working to get them addressed), you can still adjust the meeting format to reduce harm:

- Shift to group check-ins if individual sessions consistently stall on shared blockers. A team standup may surface that everyone is hitting the same wall, which makes the systemic nature undeniable.

- Move tactical updates async and reserve live time for conversations that benefit from back-and-forth dialogue. Don't waste precious face time on status reports.

- Change the frequency if the current cadence is creating pressure without value. Sometimes, less frequent but more substantive conversations work better than weekly check-ins that feel forced.

- Be honest about what the meeting can and can't do. "I know there are frustrations here that go beyond what we can solve in this conversation. I want you to know I see that, and I'm working on it at a different level."

The key principle: never fully eliminate a connection without replacement. Even if the format changes, maintain the relationship. The goal is to serve psychological needs, not to satisfy a checklist.

KEY TAKEAWAY:

When one-on-ones consistently fail despite good technique, the meeting isn't the problem. It's a diagnostic signal. Remember: See it. Say it. Scale it. See the pattern in your meetings. Say it out loud, name what you're observing. Scale the conversation to the organizational level, because some problems can't be fixed in a conference room. Don't put tape over the dashboard. Look under the hood.

CHAPTER TEN

THE POCKET PLAYBOOK

Your Quick-Reference Toolkit

This chapter is designed to be torn out, photocopied, or saved to your phone. Everything you need on a few pages. Use it before meetings. Reference it when something's not working. Share it with your team.

But remember what this book has taught: the techniques matter less than the psychology behind them. Every practice here is designed to feed Autonomy, Competence, or Relatedness. When something isn't working, ask which need isn't being met. When something works beautifully, ask which need is being fed.

And when good technique still produces bad results, the meeting isn't the problem. It's a signal. Look under the hood.

THE CORE FRAMEWORK: THREE PSYCHOLOGICAL NEEDS

- AUTONOMY — The need to feel in control of one's own life. *Fed by:* Employee-led openings, co-created solutions, choice in development. *Undermined by:* Micromanagement, approval bottlenecks, and dictated solutions.
- COMPETENCE — The need to feel capable and effective. *Fed by:* Specific recognition, visibility of progress, connection to purpose. *Undermined by:* Vague feedback, broken tools, unclear expectations.
- RELATEDNESS — The need to feel connected to others. *Fed by:* Consistent presence, kept commitments, genuine attention. *Undermined by:* Canceled meetings, broken promises, distracted listening.

MEETING STRUCTURE (30-60 MINUTES)

1. EMPLOYEE-LED OPENING (10 min): They walk through their prepared items: wins, blockers, concerns. Their agenda, not yours. *Feeds Autonomy.*
2. ALIGNMENT CHECK (5 min): Connect their work to team objectives. Review progress on action items from last meeting. *Feeds Competence.*

3. FEEDBACK & DEVELOPMENT (10 min): Three sustains, three improves, co-create solutions. *Feeds Competence (sustains) and Autonomy (co-creation).*

4. ACTION ITEMS & CLOSE (5 min): Summarize commitments with owners and deadlines. Ask: "Anything we didn't cover?" Confirm next meeting. *Feeds Relatedness.*

THE SUSTAIN-IMPROVE FRAMEWORK

Sustains first. Three specific things working well. Be specific: "Your client updates have reduced their anxiety," not "Good communication." This feeds Competence and creates receptivity.

Improves second. Three growth areas, framed as process, not personality. Future-focused: "Going forward..." not "You always..." Future framing activates problem-solving, not defense.

Co-create solutions. "What's your plan? How can I support?" Let them own the fix. This feeds Autonomy and creates ownership.

"Sustains aren't the appetizer. They're the main course. Recognition creates the receptivity that allows feedback to land."

MEETING CADENCE BY ROLE

- Individual Contributors: Weekly, 30 minutes. Focus on blockers, tactical progress, and personal development. Weekly catches Competence-thwarting early.
- Managers/Directors: Bi-weekly, 45 minutes. Focus on team health, leadership challenges, and cascading priorities. Bi-weekly respects their Autonomy while maintaining connection.
- Executives: Monthly or quarterly, 60 minutes. Focus on strategic alignment, candid feedback, and blind spots. Less frequent but substantive feeds Relatedness without overwhelming.

PREPARATION CHECKLIST

Before the meeting: Agenda shared 24 hours ahead (removes threat through clarity). Review notes from the last meeting (show continuity and feed Relatedness). Identify 3 sustains and 3 improves (preparation enables recognition). Flag any difficult topics in advance (no ambushes).

After the meeting: Send a recap within 24 hours (signals priority, builds trust). Document action items with owners and deadlines. Update progress log (makes development visible, feeds Competence). Set agenda items for next meeting (creates continuity).

RED FLAGS: WHEN THE MEETING ISN'T THE PROBLEM

Good technique, bad results? The meeting is the signal, not the problem.

- Same blockers keep resurfacing. The system is stuck, not the person.
- Venting without progress. They've learned that raising concerns changes nothing.
- Consistent reschedules or dread. They've learned that showing up vulnerable gets punished.
- Sustains land, improves trigger shutdown. Feedback has been weaponized before.
- Low energy despite good structure. The work has lost its meaning.

If these patterns show up across multiple employees, stop fixing the meeting. See it. Say it. Scale it. The problem is organizational.

SIMPLE TOOLS THAT WORK

A shared Google Doc or OneNote per direct report. Update after each meeting. Easy to reference, easy to search.

For larger teams: Slack/Teams channels for quick recaps. Asana or Notion for action item tracking.

Keep it simple. The best system is the one you'll actually use. Elaborate systems get abandoned. Simple systems persist.

START HERE

Pick one direct report. Schedule a 30-minute meeting for this week. Send an agenda 24 hours before. Run it using the structure above. Send a recap within 24 hours after.

Do this consistently for one month. Notice what changes. Then ask: Where else?

- Where else does ambiguity create threat?
- Where else do commitments get forgotten?
- Where else does the sequence of conversation matter?
- Where else are psychological needs being missed?

The one-on-one is where you learn these principles. The organization is where you apply them.

FOR LEADERS ROLLING THIS OUT

Share this playbook with your managers. Run a 30-minute session walking through the structure. Have them practice together before using it with their teams.

Start with a pilot. One team, one month. Track what changes: Are meetings happening consistently? Are action items getting completed? Is feedback flowing in both directions? Are patterns emerging that suggest organizational issues?

Once the pilot works, expand. Make shared meeting notes part of your performance review process. The documentation creates accountability and continuity.

Watch for systemic patterns. If multiple managers report the same red flags, the problem isn't technique. Use the one-on-one data as an organizational diagnostic. What's the check engine light revealing?

THE PRINCIPLE BEHIND THE PRACTICE

These meetings work when they serve the people in them. Structure creates safety. Consistency builds trust. Follow-through turns talk into action.

But the deeper principle is this: humans are intrinsically motivated when their psychological needs are met. Autonomy, Competence, Relatedness. We don't have to add motivation. We have to stop thwarting it.

"The one-on-one is the smallest unit of organizational relationship. Get it right, and you've created a pocket where psychological needs are fed. Scale that pocket, and you've changed the culture."

The tools are simple. The habit takes practice. The impact compounds.

Start this week.

KEY TAKEAWAY:

Four sections. Thirty minutes. Agenda before, recap after.

But the structure isn't the point: the psychology is. Every practice either feeds or thwarts Autonomy, Competence, or Relatedness.

When something's not working, ask which need is being neglected. When patterns persist across employees, stop fixing the meeting. See it. Say it. Scale it.

And always ask: *where else?*

THE ARC SELF-ASSESSMENT

*Measuring Organizational Friction
Against Psychological Needs*

This assessment measures how well your organization supports the three core psychological needs: Autonomy, Relatedness, and Competence (ARC).

Answer based on your honest observations of your team or organization. If you manage others, answer from the perspective of what your direct reports experience. If you're unsure, go with your first instinct.

The goal isn't a perfect score. It's clarity about where friction exists.

For each statement, rate your level of agreement:

1 = Strongly Disagree | 2 = Disagree |
3 = Neutral | 4 = Agree | 5 = Strongly Agree

SECTION 1: AUTONOMY *The need to feel in control of one's own work and decisions.*

1. Employees have meaningful input into how their work gets done. ____
2. Employees can make routine decisions without seeking approval. ____
3. Employees set their own priorities within their areas of responsibility. ____
4. Employees can adjust their schedules based on their own judgment. ____
5. Employees understand how decisions that affect them are made. ____
6. When employees raise concerns, those concerns influence outcomes. ____
7. Approval processes are proportionate to the decisions being made. ____
8. Policies assume good faith rather than requiring proof of it. ____

Autonomy Subtotal: ____ / 40

SECTION 2: RELATEDNESS *The need to feel connected to others and part of something larger.*

1. Scheduled meetings happen consistently without frequent cancellation. ____

2. Commitments made in meetings are tracked and kept. ____

3. Announced initiatives are followed through to completion. ____

4. Managers know their direct reports beyond their work output. ____

5. Interactions include time for connection that is not task-focused. ____

6. Teams maintain stable membership over time. ____

7. Employees can voice concerns without fear of negative consequences. ____

8. Employees can admit mistakes without fear of punishment. ____

Relatedness Subtotal: ____ / 40

SECTION 3: COMPETENCE *The need to feel capable, effective, and growing.*

1. Employees receive specific recognition for what they do well. ____

2. Feedback focuses on future improvement rather than past failure. ____

3. Employees can see their own progress and development over time. ____

4. Internal tools and systems support rather than hinder work. ____

5. Employees can connect their daily work to organizational purpose. ____

6. Expectations are clear and stable over reasonable timeframes. ____

7. Professional development is treated as investment in capability. ____

8. Employees can complete tasks without procedural obstacles. ____

Competence Subtotal: ____ / 40

SCORING
TOTAL ARC SCORE: ____ / 120

INTERPRETING YOUR SCORE

- 96-120: Strong Foundation. Your organization generally supports psychological needs. One-on-one techniques should produce strong results. Focus on refinement and consistency.

- 72-95: Mixed Signals. Some needs are being met, others neglected. One-on-ones may work inconsistently. Look at which section scored lowest. That's where organizational friction is concentrated.

- 48-71: Significant Friction. The environment is actively working against psychological needs. One-on-one techniques will help but cannot overcome systemic issues. The meeting is the check engine light. Time to look under the hood.

- Below 48: Critical. The organization is systematically thwarting psychological needs. Individual meeting technique cannot fix this. Intervention is needed at the organizational level.

Which section scored lowest?

That's your primary friction point.

Low Autonomy: You may be over-controlling. Look for approval bottlenecks, micromanagement patterns, and policies that assume bad faith.

Low Relatedness: Your organization may be transactional rather than connected. Look for broken commitments, isolation patterns, and efficiency that crowds out connection.

Low Competence: Your organization may be making capable people feel ineffective. Look for obstructive tools, unclear expectations, and feedback that punishes rather than develops.

The score isn't the point. The clarity is. Now you know where to look.

Visit **ketchumadvisory.com/arc** to take this assessment online. You'll receive your scores with personalized interpretation and recommendations based on your friction profile.

WHEN THE MEETING ISN'T THE PROBLEM

This book gave you tools for better one-on-ones. But sometimes the meeting isn't the problem. It's the signal.

If your ARC Self-Assessment revealed significant friction across multiple employees, if good technique consistently produces disappointing results, the intervention needed isn't at the meeting level. It's at the organizational level.

THE THREE DIAGNOSTIC INDICES

At Ketchum Advisory, we measure organizational friction using three indices:

The Infantilization Index (Autonomy): Where is the organization treating adults like children? Approval chains for trivial decisions, keystroke monitoring, policies that assume bad faith.

The insight: Trust is cheaper than control. Usually, the control costs 10x more than the risk it's preventing.

The Stupidity Index (Competence): Where do tools and processes make smart people feel stupid? Clunky software, endless inconclusive meetings, bureaucratic friction that blocks completion. The insight: People enjoy work when they feel good at it. Systems that make capable people feel helpless kill Competence, and motivation crashes accordingly.

The Loneliness Index (Relatedness): Where does the organization prioritize transaction over connection? Email instead of conversation, efficiency metrics that punish socialization, constant reorganization that prevents stable bonds. The insight: Some "waste" is actually investment in the human fabric that makes collaboration possible.

THE RETENTION FRICTION AUDIT

For organizations ready to address friction at scale, we offer a diagnostic service called the Retention Friction Audit. Here's what it includes:

- Document and policy review (approval thresholds, meeting structures, feedback systems)
- Structured interviews across role levels using the protocol in this book
- Scoring on all three indices with specific policy-level findings

- Prioritized action plan: what to stop doing, what to change, what to protect
- Delivered within 10 business days

THE PROMISE

Organizations that implement three or more priority recommendations typically see measurable improvement in engagement metrics within 60 days. If you implement and don't see movement, we re-engage at no cost to identify what we missed.

WHO THIS IS FOR

The audit is designed for founders and CEOs of small and medium-sized businesses who are experiencing scaling friction: good people leaving, cultural misalignment with new hires, declining energy as processes become bureaucratic.

It's not for organizations looking for another engagement survey. It's not for leadership teams unwilling to change policy based on findings. And it's not for companies that want to "add motivation programs" rather than remove the barriers blocking motivation that's already there.

WHAT YOU WON'T GET

- Engagement surveys that sit in a drawer
- Motivation programs layered on demotivating policies

- Generic "culture transformation" promises
- Anything that requires you to trust us more than you trust your own data

NEXT STEP

If the ARC Self-Assessment showed you have an organizational friction problem, the audit will show you exactly where it lives and what to do about it.

Visit **ketchumadvisory.co** to schedule a 30-minute diagnostic call. No pitch, just a conversation to determine whether the audit is the right fit for your situation.

The one-on-one is where you learn the principles. The organization is where you apply them.

ABOUT THE AUTHOR

Pete Ketchum is an industrial-organizational psychologist and the founder of Ketchum Advisory. Before studying what makes people tick, he spent years in roles where reading people was the job: military interrogation, prison de-escalation, state trooper. Each taught him that trust isn't built through authority. It's built through structure, consistency, and follow-through. He later held leadership positions across finance, construction, and tech, where he discovered that most corporate "best practices" work against human psychology rather than with it.

Ketchum Advisory helps founders and executives navigate growth transitions. The hands-on instincts that built the company don't always scale with it. We take a scientific approach to systematizing what makes the organization unique, so it can grow without losing what makes it special.

Learn more at **ketchumadvisory.co** or **peteketchum.com**